D1535920

Suzanne W. Roche/Oak Lei Press

Kidding Around NYC/Suzanne W. Roche - 1st ed.
ISBN 978-0-9961484-2-9

NEW YORK CITY

We know what you're thinking—

the birthplace of Scrabble and toilet paper, home to George Washington's tooth and Einstein's eyeballs. Or maybe you like to think of it as the place where Americans got their first taste of ice cream cones, delicatessens, and pizza.

But trust us, there's more to New York CIty! If you want to discover what else makes the city so special, this book is for you.

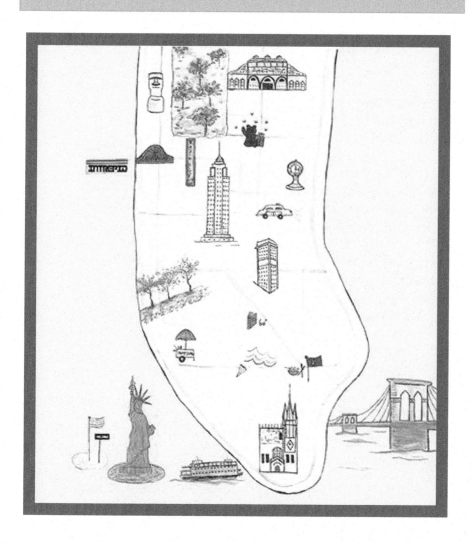

THE STOPS

NEW YORK ON THE SQUARE   6
In The Know   7
Subways   10
Times Square   12
Chrysler Building   13
Food Carts   14
Grand Central Terminal   15
The Big Apple   17
Taxis   17
Wall Street   18

GO DOWN IN HISTORY   19
Ellis Island   21
Tenement Museum   24
Merchant's House   25
Flatiron Building   26
Trinity Church   28

MUST-SEE MUSEUMS   30
American Museum of Natural History (AMNH)   30
Metropolitan Museum of Art (Met)   34
Museum of Modern Art (MOMA)   37

THINGS ARE LOOKING UP   38
Statue of Liberty   38
Empire State Building   40
One World Trade Center   44
Rockefeller Center   46

ALL THE WORLD'S A STAGE   49
Broadway   49
Radio City Music Hall   50
New York City Ballet (NYCB)   51
Big Apple Circus   52
Museum of the Moving Image   53

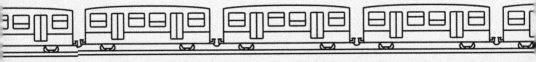

A WALK IN THE PARK   **54**
Central Park   54
Prospect Park   57
High Line Park   58

JUST ADD WATER   **60**
Brooklyn Bridge   60
Intrepid   62
Staten Island Ferry   63

GO WILD!   **64**
Bronx Zoo   64
Central Park Zoo   66
New York Public Library   67

PLAY BY PLAY   **68**

'TIS THE SEASON   **71**

WHERE IN NEW YORK WOULD YOU FIND THESE?   **72**

ANSWERS TO YOUR QUESTIONS   **73**

GLOSSARY   **74**

LOCATION, LOCATION, LOCATION   **75**

I'LL BE READING YOU   **76**

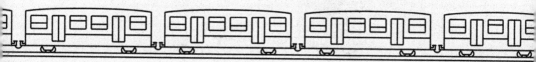

In The Know

Times Square

Subways

Chrysler Building

Food Carts

Grand Central Terminal

The Big Apple

Taxis

Wall Street

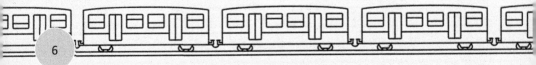

New York City might not have everything, but it has a lot. We aren't just talking about George Washington's tooth either (although it was the only real one he had left when he was inaugurated as President in New York in 1789 so that does make it pretty special). We're talking about a lot more.

In fact, the only word to describe the city is: bustling-bright-lively-breathtaking-memorable-dynamic-unlike-any-other. (You though we were going to say something like "cool" or "fun," didn't you?)

Here is New York City (NYC), at the bottom of New York State

Did you know NYC has the largest subway system in North America? That it keeps over thirteen thousand taxis busy and receives over fifty million visitors a year? It houses 25% of the world's gold bullion? For almost one hundred years, it's been one of the largest consumers of helium in the country?*

* For that last one, can you guess why? We aren't going to parade the answer in front of you but we might give you a hint that will balloon into an answer (you'll find the answer to this and other questions throughout the book on page 73).

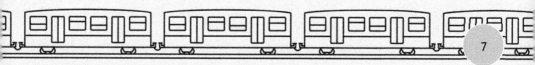

Skyscrapers (only Hong Kong has more), headquarters of businesses, world politics, fine arts and cuisine, great parks and small neighborhoods, oyster beds, and beaver lodges (yes, you read that correctly). Throughout its history, NYC has had a colorful variety of inhabitants.

Today, so many people of different nationalities live in the city that over 800 languages are spoken (it would take a person over a half-hour just to say "hello" in all those languages!).

And to think, it all started on the island of Manhattan close to four hundred years ago. Then in 1895, four surrounding areas joined the island to become New York City and make it the second largest city in the world (only London was larger at the time). Even today, NYC is one of the biggest cities in the world.

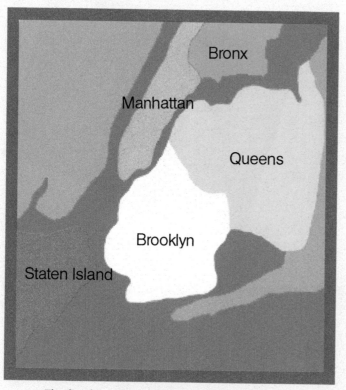

The five boroughs that make up New York City

You don't need Einstein's eyeballs to see New York City is a place with a lot going on!

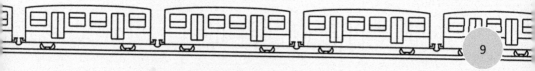

Subways have been running through NYC for over one hundred years. As the city grew, a trip across town was no longer a short walk; it could take a large part of a day to get from one end of the crowded city to the other (some people like to joke that it's still that way).

Until the 1900s, public transportation was made up of stage-coaches and a few elevated trains. But it was clear New York needed something that could cover the growing city, and the streets weren't up to the task.

It's amazing that it ever got built: the tunnels had to run below a massive city and operate amongst an underground maze of gas and electrical lines, sewers, building foundations, and rivers.

Early subway construction around 1900

When the system was done in 1904, New York had a subway with over nine miles of tracks going to twenty-eight stations.

Today, the subway system has over 450 stations and approximately 660 miles of track*. The trains go just about everywhere throughout the boroughs— and they do it all day, every day.

Over 5 million people ride the subways every day so you aren't always guaranteed a seat!

* That is enough track to go from New York to South Carolina!

If there is one place that proves New York is a city of nonstop energy and activity, it's Time Square.

It's busy day...

Throughout the years, as American entertainment grew (with burlesque, vaudeville, musical theater, and motion pictures), Times Square changed from a quiet business center into one of the most famous entertainment districts in the world.

The area is a whirlwind of energy, day or night—because if you can't be loud and flashy in Times Square, then where can you? It's fitting that Times Square hosts the city's annual New Year's celebration. It's a tradition that began in the early 1900s and now attracts a million people each December 31st.

or night

No matter what time of year though, don't go if you want some quiet time alone—over 350,000 people a day visit!

 TOKEN TRIVIA

Times Square got its name from the *New York Times*. The newspaper moved its offices from downtown to 42nd Street, which was then called Longacre Square. The building now has the address of One Times Square.

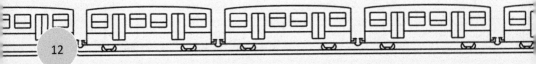

When the Chrysler Building was constructed in 1929, it was in a race to be the tallest building in NYC. (Can you guess its rival?)

Walter Chrysler came to town with plans to build his car company headquarters. Soon, that wasn't enough. He decided he also wanted to have the tallest building in the city. Much of the planning (and even construction) was done in secret. The famous spire was built outside the city. Its four sections were secretly brought into the city and installed on top of the building in ninety minutes (is it any wonder people think NYC is fast-paced?).

Upon its completion in May 1930, the Chrysler Building was officially the tallest skyscraper in the world (for a whopping eleven months).

Sure it was a short reign, but many people decided being tall isn't everything. This building speaks to the lavish taste of an era. With its art deco design, shiny spire, and eagle heads (taken from Chrysler 's automobile designs), the Chrysler Building is a lasting reminder of the glamour and excitement that defined the 1920s.

FOOD CARTS

Street food and food carts are as old as the city. As far back as the 1600s, people sold clams, oysters, and corn on the cob around the streets on New York. At one point, NYC had more oyster beds than anywhere else in the world!

As more immigrants came to the city, more peddlers set up carts on neighborhood streets that offered familiar foods to them. You can still find carts selling pickles, knishes, and sausage, as they did long ago.

Today, food carts have branched out in both their locations and their menus. Especially around the crowded business areas, they line the streets at lunch time, offering just about any kind of food you can imagine (okay, maybe not clams anymore).

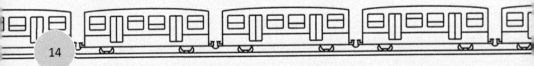

GRAND CENTRAL TERMINAL

This beautiful one hundred-year old train terminal is the largest in the world, and sees more than 750,000 people travel through it a day. It's hard to believe much of it was almost destroyed by developers in the 1960s.

That plan changed when Jacqueline Kennedy Onassis stepped in. Between her fame and the public's support, Grand Central was named a National Historic Landmark, and the city got to work restoring the terminal to its original beauty.

Grand Central Depot

When Grand Central Depot was built on in 1871, it was the size of two football fields. The public might have loved this new addition if the steam trains didn't sound so loud, smell really bad, and spew soot. The tracks north of the depot were moved underground and everyone figured the problem was solved.

No such luck. It actually got worse. Now the city had dangerous, dark, smog-filled tunnels. In 1902, two trains crashed when a driver couldn't see through all the soot. It was clear the city needed electric trains and a station that could serve them. The result was Grand Central Terminal.

Do you know? What's the difference between a train <u>terminal</u> and a train <u>station</u>?

SECRETS OF GRAND CENTRAL TERMINAL

Beneath the famous clock is a secret staircase down to the lower level of the terminal. Passengers are not allowed to use it (or see it).

Hitler had plans to destroy the terminal during World War II. Two German spies made it to the coast of Long Island before they were caught. Their mission was to destroy the power plants located on the secret M42 level beneath Grand Central.

President Franklin D. Roosevelt had his own secret track, #61, that could take him from Grand Central up to the Waldorf Astoria Hotel without anyone seeing him.

On the lower level is the "Whispering Gallery," where you can stand at one end of the room (facing one of the arched ceiling supports) and hear someone whispering from the opposite end of the room. They'll sound as if they are standing right beside you.

The beautiful ceiling, painted in 1913, shows constellations in the sky but (oops) the artist painted it backwards.

TOKEN TRIVIA

Years of grime were removed from the waiting room ceiling during the restoration. A small patch was left so you can see how dirty it actually was. Can you guess the main culprit? Cigarette smoke!

In the 1950s, the government wanted to display a rocket in the main waiting room. It proved it to be a bad idea. During the installation, the rocket turned out to be too tall and poked a hole in the ceiling.

Grand Central Station is next door to the terminal. It's the post office!

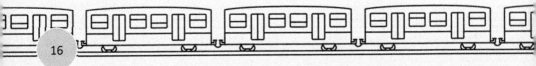

THE BIG APPLE

Do you ever wonder how New York City got the nickname, "The Big Apple?"

If you're not sure, you're not alone. It could come from the state fruit, an apple, or from the apple-sellers on the streets in the 1930s. Maybe it was the jazz musicians, who used the phrase to explain where they were playing. Then there was a jazz club called "The Big Apple."

A lot of people have studied this and most believe now that it came from horse racing. The big prizes won in the races around the city were called "big apples." The term soon came to mean capturing the ultimate jackpot: New York City, of course!

TAXIS

How can you tell if a cab is available?

Look at the lights on the roof.

If the center light is lit, the cab is available so go ahead and hail it.

If the lights are off, look for another cab. This one already has a passenger.

If the "off duty" light is lit—you guessed it—the driver is done working for the day and is not taking any more passengers. Don't worry though: there are a lot more cabs around to hail!

There are over 12,000 taxis in New York, which is a good thing because they are a popular way for people to get around.

What began as a wall to protect Dutch settlers from the British is now one of the most powerful financial centers in the world.

The wall itself was taken down, but the road that ran beside it was kept. Very little brainstorming probably went on when it was time to name the street (Wall Street, get it?).

The surrounding area of Wall Street had always been used for business and trade. As business grew and formalized in the city, it was a natural choice for establishing a stock exchange. Today, Wall Street is the home of the New York Stock Exchange, as well as the headquarters of many financial firms.

The Federal Reserve has a vault on Wall Street that is eighty feet underground but has no doors! Stored inside is about one-quarter of the world's gold bullion.

The vault is built on bedrock to support the enormous weight of all the gold. It currently weighs over 6,700 tons.

Wall Street in the 1800s

How many Statues of Liberty would you need to equal 6,700 tons? 20? 30? More?

GO DOWN IN HISTORY

NYC has been a popular place to live for hundreds of years. While the Native Americans liked to hunt in Manhattan, the Dutch arrived in 1624 with a different idea. Anyone who wanted to get rich in the New World had to have some skin in the game (in the form of pelts, that is).

The British arrive in New Amsterdam

It all had to do with the island's location, at the mouth of the Hudson River. It was the perfect gateway for trade (and if there was one thing European countries cared about at that point in history, it was trade).

The Dutch wasted no time in buying the land from the Native Americans, paying them 60 guilders* in equipment and supplies. The healthy population of beavers living around Manhattan wasn't so lucky and, very quickly, the Dutch became rich exporting beaver pelts to Europe.

New York City in the 1700s

* That's worth a little over $7,000 today. You can't even buy a new car for that. Forget about trying to buy a city!

The European settlers named their city New Amsterdam and, almost immediately, had to fend off other countries interested in controlling the valuable land. (Didn't we say it was a popular place?)

The Dutch surrender to the British

In 1664, the British sent the Duke of York (the brother of the King of England) with war ships to seize control of New Amsterdam. After a surprisingly uneventful confrontation, the Dutch surrendered the city and the English took over. One of the first items of business was changing its name—to New York, of course!

The NYC skyline in the 1700s

New York changed hands, one final time, during the Revolutionary War when the Colonists took it from the British. For one year, in 1789, it was even the capital of the new United States. Do you know what other cities were our country's capital?

ELLIS ISLAND

Ellis Island was our country's busiest immigration station for much of the twentieth century. More than 12 million people arrived here with the hope of making a new life for themselves and their families.

In the early 1900s, most of the immigrants came from Europe. They were trying to escape extreme poverty, religious bigotry, and unjust governments, all which left thousands of people without jobs or food. These families believed they would have no chance of prospering (or even surviving) if they stayed in their homelands. Many people had heard that America was different. It was known as a country where anyone could become a success if they worked hard enough.

 TOKEN TRIVIA

Part of the island is actually in New Jersey.

The island was made larger with landfill from the city's subway and Grand Central Terminal excavations.

The first person who immigrated through Ellis Island was a fifteen-year-old Irish girl, Annie Moore. She was with her two younger brothers. The city gave her a ten-dollar gold piece as a congratulations.

Outside the station was a pillar where family and friends waited for their newly arrived loved ones to exit the building. It was nicknamed "the kissing post."

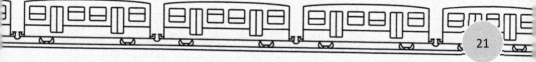

Going through the immigration process on Ellis Island was simple for some people. For most immigrants though, it was long and tiring, sometimes even heartbreaking. It all depended on what a person's passenger class was on their arriving ship. Follow the path that immigrants took to enter America:

START HERE

A doctor comes on board the ship to examine you

You just spent many LONG weeks on a ship. Your first view of America is the New York sky-line and the Statue of Liberty. In what class did you sail? First, Second or Steerage?

First or Second

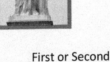

The Luggage Room

Steerage

An immigrant family arrives

You take a barge over to Ellis Is-land (you might have to wait hours or even days for your turn)

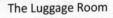

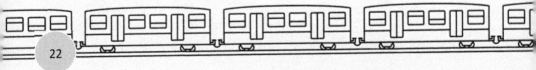

WELCOME TO AMERICA!

Ill? You're quarantined until you are well

Healthy? You are free to go

Answering questions in the Registry Room

The six-second exam

You leave all your luggage outside and follow others up the staircase. Watch out! Doctors watch to see if anyone is too sick to keep up

Healthy? You go to the Registry Room and answer questions about yourself. Afterwards, you are free to go

You enter the Great Hall and have a "six second" exam by a doctor

Ill? You are either quarantined until you are well or <u>sent</u> <u>back</u> to the country you just left

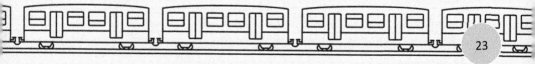

In the early part of the twentieth century, millions of people immigrated to America. Most of these people made their new homes in large cities. A place like New York gave immigrants the support of an ethnic community, and offered a lot of manual jobs for people who didn't speak English yet.

New immigrants in New York often lived in tenements. So many people moved to America in such a short time that it was hard to fit everyone. In the early 1900s, more than half of the people living in New York made their homes in these crowded buildings and neighborhoods.

A visit to the Tenement Museum lets you see what life was like for these families. Inside this building, there were sixteen apartments (at one time there had been twenty two), and you can learn how many large families made do in these very small flats.

You can also "meet" immigrants who once lived here. They can answer any questions you have about life in New York back then.

 TOKEN TRIVIA

For a long time, there was no electricity, indoor plumbing or toilets in the buildings.

Several families often lived together or took in boarders.

Many apartments only had one bedroom, which meant that the children shared beds or slept on other furniture in the front room.

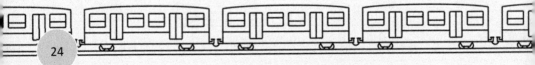

MERCHANT'S HOUSE

Merchant's House is now a museum but it once was the home of a hardware merchant, Seabury Tredwell, and his family.

Inside, it looks exactly like it did 150 years ago so you can see how he lived with his wife and eight children. All the furnished rooms are full of artwork, clothing, and decorations that belonged to the family.

Many people say they have seen more than just belongings when they visit. Gertrude Tredwell, the last living Tredwell, spent her entire life here (being born and dying in the same bed!) and is said to wander through the rooms, watching over her home. It's no coincidence that Merchant's House has been called "the most haunted house in the city."

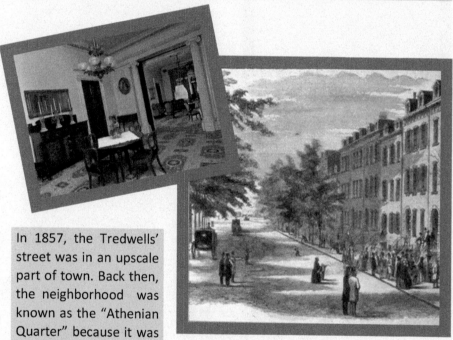

In 1857, the Tredwells' street was in an upscale part of town. Back then, the neighborhood was known as the "Athenian Quarter" because it was so sophisticated.

The Bond Street area in 1857

The house is located in what used to be known as the Bond Street Area. Long ago, this area was considered the suburbs of New York City!

The Flatiron Building isn't just a funny-looking, skinny building. Its design structure changed the way cities expanded. It was the country's first skyscraper and inspired future architects to build in a new dimension (up!).

When it was built, the Flatiron was considered one of the tallest and most unusual buildings in the city. At 285 feet tall, it doesn't come close to being one of NY's tallest skyscrapers—but it still is the most unusual.

At the turn of the 20th century, the city was trying to move businesses out of the crowded area of Wall Street. But when they hired Daniel Burnham, an architect trained in the Chicago School of Architecture, to design the new building, more would change than just the neighborhood.

Until now, buildings were constructed of heavy stone and brick, which made for thick walls and small windows. The ideas Burnham used were new: build on a steel frame that could bear the weight rather than relying on the walls.

Burnham's steel design allowed for a taller building with more space inside (since the walls could be thinner) and include more windows, so there would be more natural light inside.

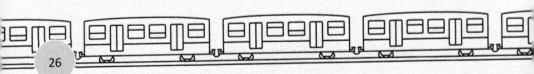

The building is triangular and shaped like a slice of pizza. At its most narrow angle, it measures only six feet across.

Early on, people worried that the Flatiron wouldn't last long. They were sure its shape weakened the building, and it would not be able to withstand the strong winds in the area. People took to calling the project "Burnham's folly." They were wrong! The building has stood for over one hundred years, proving you don't have to be huge to be strong!

Even though the building was originally called the Fuller Building, the name "Flatiron" seems more fitting, don't you think?

The namesake

 TOKEN TRIVIA:

The Flatiron Building faces the grave of a Civil War veteran (the monument is on 25th Street between 5th Avenue and Broadway). It's the only building in New York that does.

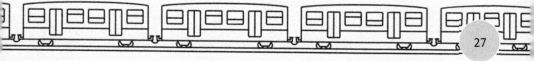

TRINITY CHURCH

Trinity Church is famous for its beauty—but also for managing to stand its ground among the busy, ever-changing skyscrapers and office buildings of the Wall Street area. That's no small feat!

St. Paul's Chapel, which is part of Trinity Church, opened in 1766. The parish itself has been around since 1697, after the British took control of the island.

This church, consecrated in 1846, is actually the third Trinity Church. The first one was destroyed in a fire and the second one in a winter storm.

Trinity Church is so old that even George Washington worshiped here!

George Washington's pew

 TOKEN TRIVIA

The oldest gravestones in the city are here. Some are over 400 years old!

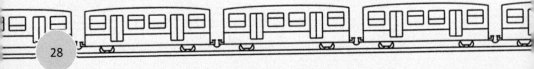

In the years before the American Revolution, the Trinity Church Parish was required to pay the British Crown rent. Can you guess how much the rent was? One peppercorn! (you were going to guess that, weren't you?)

INVOICE

FOR ANNUAL RENT

TOTAL DUE UPON RECEIPT:

1 PEPPERCORN

The term "peppercorns" was actually used to mean any small amount of money to be paid. But when Queen Elizabeth II visited New York in 1976, she was paid for hundreds of back rent with real peppercorns (the kind you grind to make a seasoning).

276 PEPPERCORNS!

 TOKEN TRIVIA

The famous pirate Captain Kidd was a parishioner at Trinity Church. He even contributed to the building of the Church! This, of course, was before he was sent to prison, put on trial, found guilty, and hanged.

Early on, people congregated outside the church to celebrate New Year's Eve. Because of all the noise they made, the tradition was stopped in 1894. When the employees of the *New York Times* moved their offices uptown, they took the celebration with them to Times Square, where it remains today.

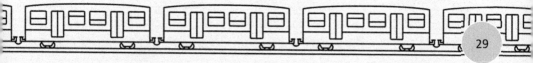

MUST-SEE MUSEUMS
AMERICAN MUSEUM OF NATURAL HISTORY (AMNH)

If you like science, the AMNH is the place for you! And if you don't like science, you just might change your mind after a visit here.

The AMNH is the largest natural history museum in the world, with over 32 million artifacts. You can examine specimens from prehistoric times and the deepest oceans, meet rock stars, big and small, and even take an accelerated journey through evolution.

Be sure to watch *The Known Universe*. You'll travel from the Himalayas through space, past the Milky Way, and out to the end of the known universe. Lucky for you, it's a round-trip journey so you'll still be able to visit the rest of the museum afterwards.

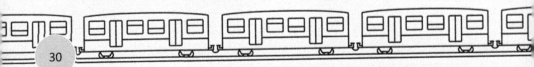

There's so much to see!

IMAX Theater

Rose Center for
Earth and Space

Fossil Hall

Hayden
Planetarium

Gemstones

Star of India

Butterfly
Conservatory

Dioramas

Don't forget the Discovery Room for kids.

The Star of India is a 563-carat star sapphire that was formed 2 billion years ago. It is so rare that is shows asterisms—or starlike figures in the reflected light—on both sides.

The Star of India

In the Akeley Hall of African Mammals, there is a chipmunk hidden in one of the dioramas. See if you can spot him when you are there.

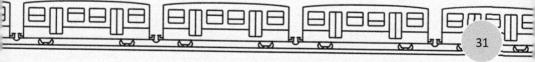

When you're at AMNH, don't miss:

The Milstein Hall of Ocean Life

You can view hundreds of sea creatures from eight different ecosystems, everything from kelp forests to the coral reefs. And it won't take long to see what hangs out in a place like this—a life-size blue whale, of course.

The Earth and Planetary Sciences

See how rocks and minerals—rare, small, common, or mammoth—together give us clues into the earth's history and the greater universe.

This ninety-four foot model of a blue whale got a makeover. Not only were the fins and flukes corrected, but the whale also got a bright paint job and a brand-new belly button.

When you visit, see if you can find out the life span of blue whales. While you're at it, try to figure out the whale's closest relative.

In the Hall of Meteorites, you can see the Ahnighito, the largest meteorite shown anywhere in the world.

To support this 34-ton specimen (it weighs more than 60,000 soccer balls!), extra braces had to be built into the bedrock under the museum.

See if you can learn the difference between a meteor and a meteorite.

The Roosevelt Rotunda

The museum has the world's largest collection of dinosaur fossils. Just as impressive, most of the dinosaurs you see have been recreated with real fossil bones rather than casts!

See if you can discover the country where most of these bones were found.

The Rose Center for Earth and Space

You can walk through the universe, see how different "big" and "little" really are, and be part of the Big Bang.

In the Heilbrunn Cosmic Pathway, you can take a tour through evolution. If you think your grandparents are old, wait until you learn about quasars.

The Tyrannosaurus Rex has a new way of looking at things, and scientists now believe it wasn't such an upstanding fellow. In the end (as in "tail"), maybe the T-Rex didn't like to get dirty.

Scientists don't like to use words like "tiny" and "huge" to describe size. Learn what they mean by "nano" and "giga" and all the other words that fit in between.

The right way

The wrong way

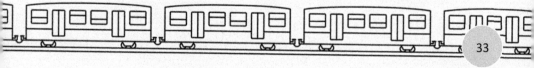

The Met is not your average museum. It is like walking into a universe of art (with gravitational pull provided at the entrance). The Met is one of the greatest art museums in the world and the largest in the United States. It has over 2 million items in its collection!

Whether you want to explore ancient Greek art, modern art, or anything in between, the Met has plenty to offer. Not only can you see traditional art forms like painting, sculpture, and photography, but you can have fun discovering new forms like armor, architecture, musical instruments, and costumes.

Washington Crossing the Delaware is the largest painting at the Met. It shows George Washington and his troops heading to the Battle of Trenton during the Revolutionary War.

The painting is 149 inches by 255 inches. You would need to spread out over 500 of these books to cover that space!

The Temple of Dendur stood beside the Nile River in Egypt for 2,000 years.

When Egypt offered it to the United States, the temple was taken apart. With each stone numbered, they were shipped to America and reassembled here.

Only one name is inscribed on the temple. See if you can find out whose it is.

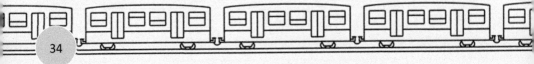

Have you ever wondered how a museum like the Met gets items for its collections? After all, they can't just go to a department store and buy them. In truth, it can be dirty work.

Curators and scholars from the Met travel around the world to participate in excavations and research. The museum is constantly taking part in archeological digs (many are going on today in the Middle East).

Of course, the museum staff does not always keep what they find. Some pieces are sent to museums within the country of the exploration, or to other countries to complete a collection. But because each discovery offers insight into past cultures and lives, everyone benefits from these projects.

This Roman sarcophagus was the first object the museum acquired in 1870. It was found in present-day Turkey.

Sarcophagi are stone coffins that were common in ancient times (some that have been found are over 2000 years old). They were usually used for important and wealthy people, and carved or painted with pictures. Most ancient cultures did not bury sarcophagi—which was probably because they weighed a ton (actually, they were closer to two tons).

 TOKEN TRIVIA:

Some works of art at the museum are so delicate that they cannot be near light, heat, or noise.

Ghost hunters have studied and explored the Met, believing many of the ancient works of art are much livelier than anyone ever imagined.

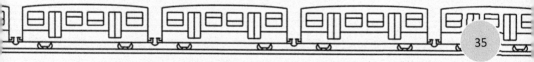

How well do you know the Met?

After you visit the museum, see if you can match the questions to the correct answers.

1. Which animal is the unofficial mascot of the Met?

2. In what book do two children run away from home and live at the Met?

3. In what collection would you find a pipa and a suzu?

4. What are The Cloisters?

5. Do any of the mummies still have bodies in them?

6. What rare card is kept at the Met?

7. What's wrong in the 1851 painting *Washington Crossing the Delaware?*

A. A museum that has European art from the Middle Ages. It's part of the Met but located further uptown.

B. A 1909 baseball card of Honus Wagner.

C. William, an Egyptian hippopotamus statue.

D. *From the Mixed-Up Files of Mrs. Basil E. Frankweiler*

E. The flag was actually not the American flag until a year later, in 1777.

F. The musical instruments, with thousands of other instruments from around the world.

G. Thirteen of them do (including one child).

Arms and Armor at the Met

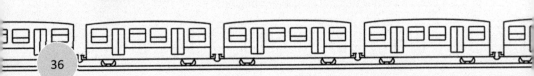

Who says modern art isn't for everyone?

The MOMA is full of art that you won't find anywhere else. Here you will see how artists express themselves with mediums that are new, surprising, and even funny.

The 1920s were a time in our history that welcomed anything "new" and "modern." In 1929, three prominent New Yorkers got together and decided the art scene in New York should be no different. With a collection of nine works of modern art, the museum opened. It was a success from the start. In fact, it has been so popular, the museum has had to move several times to accommodate its growing and changing collection that now totals over 150,000 works.

What special distinction does Matisse's *Le Bateau* hold?

Oppenheim's Object is a cup, saucer, and spoon covered in fur.

It's not only a web address, it's a silk-screen example of modern symbols.

The Statue of Liberty is one of the most well-known landmarks in the country. Since her arrival in 1886, the statue has stood as a symbol for America's independent spirit.

Following the American Civil War, France gave the statue to America as a tribute to the hopes and ideals of our country.

The sculptor, Frederic Bartholdi, modeled the "Liberty Enlightening the World" statue after *Libertas*, the Roman goddess of freedom. For more detailed inspiration, it has been said Bartholdi used his mother as his model (some might say he carried a torch for his mom).

The statue under construction in Paris

While France built the statue, the United States constructed the pedestal on which it would stand. Its location was to be on Bedloe's Island (now called Liberty Island) in New York's harbor. Before this, the island housed a military fort that had a star-shaped base. That base still remains and is now part of the statue's foundation.

A lot of people think the seven spires on the crown stands for the seven seas or seven continents. They actually symbolize the rays of the sun.

The torch stands for enlightenment. This is a replacement torch—the original, which was replaced in 1984, is displayed in the monument's lobby.

The chains at the statue's feet are broken to show that America is free.

The tablet reads "July 4, 1776," in honor of the Declaration of Independence.

 TOKEN TRIVIA:

The statue was shipped in 200 crates. The 350 pieces took four months to assemble.

The only way to get to Liberty Island is on the official ferry. Private boats are not allowed.

Winds cause parts of the statue to sway up to six inches.

The man who built the structure of the Statue of Liberty created another famous landmark in Paris, France. Do you know his name?

EMPIRE STATE BUILDING

The Empire State Building is one of New York's most famous landmarks and one of the Seven Wonders of the Modern World. Even in this city full of history and chutzpah, the Empire State Building stands out (in more ways than one).

In the 1920s, New York found itself in a race (oddly, against itself). Developers and business owners wanted to have the tallest building in the city. The owners of land on Fifth Avenue and 34th Street were bent on creating a skyscraper that would not only tower over every other structure, but become a centerpiece for the modern city of New York.

Do you know?

Who climbed up the Empire State Building but couldn't get down?

It took only two weeks to draw up plans for the new skyscraper. Then someone noticed that the building would measure only four feet higher than its competition across town, which was a very close 1,046 feet.

The property owners and builders got very creative. They decided to build a docking station for dirigibles on top. That (very short-lived) plan would bring the Empire State Building to 1,250 feet.

It was built in under fourteen months—every week, over four stories were going up! The city struggled to update its building codes to keep up with what was being created.*

Many people thought dirigibles were going to be the most popular form of air travel in the future (airplanes proved to be safer and faster).

* The city was presented with a new elevator invention. To deliver people to so many different floors, the architects designed "banks" that would allow different elevators to stop at different floors. It's the equivalent of express and local subways. Today, those elevators can whisk visitors to the eighty-sixth floor in less than a minute!

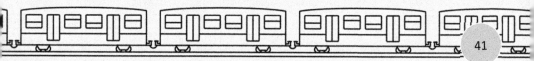

The foremen constructed a railway that could quickly bring materials from storage to the job site. The interior and the exterior were built at the same time. While the building frame was going up, the plumbing, electricity, and telephone wire were being installed inside.

Early construction of the building

Three thousand men (mostly recent immigrants) rose to the occasion and worked over 7 million man hours to construct the Empire State Building. They worked on Sundays and holidays and were paid $15 a day (an impressive amount during the Depression).

They became known as "sky boys," because their work took them hundreds of feet into the sky.

One of the sky boys

 TOKEN TRIVIA:

The Empire State Building is so big that it has its own zip code.

The building has 102 floors, 1,860 steps, and 73 elevators.

Besides all the aluminum and steel, the building is made with 10 million bricks.

Including the lightning rod*, the building now stands at 1,454 feet. That's about 323 cars piled on top of one another!

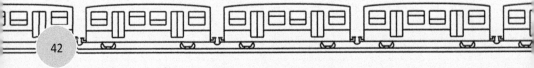

Wonder how they did it? They ran like an assembly line to keep everything moving:

The heater handled ten rivets in the forge. When the rivets were hot enough, he would use tongs to toss them (up to seventy-five feet!) to:

The catcher, who would use an old can to catch them (they were too hot to touch by hand). He'd use his tongs to place a rivet in a beam hole for:

The bucker-up, who would hold the rivet in place so that:

The gunman could use his special hammer to secure the rivet in the girder.

And remember, they had to do this for *every* beam in the 102-story building. The last rivet put on was made of solid gold—to celebrate a job well done!

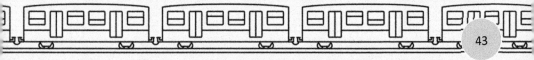

The new One World Trade Center not only heightens the beauty of the downtown skyline, it also commemorates the two buildings of the original World Trade Center, which were destroyed in the terrorist attacks on September 11, 2001.

What started as the Freedom Tower was renamed One World Trade Center before the building was completed in 2014.

It took over 1500 construction workers eight years to build the 1,776 foot tower. That number is no coincidence—the height is ascribed to another great part of American history, the signing of the Declaration of Independence.

Without the antenna on top, the building measures 1,326 feet, the height of the original North Tower of the World Trade Center. A 33 foot glass parapet along the roof brings the building to 1,368 feet, the height of the original South Tower.

The tower is now the tallest building in New York City, the United States, and North America. If that isn't enough, it's also the third tallest in the world!. How's that for a towering accomplishment!

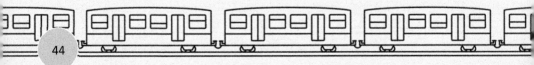

A lot of planning went into this high-reaching project. 45,000 tons of steel and 200,000 cubic yards of concrete were used in the structure. That's more than three times the concrete used in the Empire State Building!

The new observation deck opening in spring 2015, called the One World Observatory, is on the 100-102 floors of the building. It's only a sixty-second ride on the special elevators but the experience around the deck is designed to last much longer.

Also part of the complex is the September 11 Memorial and Museum. Two reflecting pools with waterfalls now fill the space once home to the original two World Trade Center buildings. The names of everyone who died in the 1993 and 2001 attacks are engraved along the pools.

The museum contains artifacts and exhibits about the events that touched millions of New Yorkers and Americans. It's a memorable and meaningful exhibition.

Today, Rockefeller Center is an office complex in midtown that is more than your average office space. The buildings and surrounding area are home to television studios, awesome city views, rooftop gardens, an ice skating rink, restaurants, a famous concert hall, and one of the city's most treasured holiday traditions. The lower plaza is lined with flags (usually those of other nations) and a statue of Prometheus decorates the center.

The story of Rockefeller Center begins in the early 1930s, when John D. Rockefeller Jr. learned that a neighborhood just south of his home was for sale. The New York Opera wanted to build their new opera house on the land. But Rockefeller, who some say disliked opera, leased the land himself.

This was a very bold move. The country was in the middle of the Great Depression and its future was uncertain. Because Rockefeller believed he could turn it into a commercial success, he agreed to pay the building's entire cost himself. Opera-lover or not, that was music to everyone's ears!

When you go up seventy stories to the Top of the Rock at Rockefeller Center, you get a great view of downtown (and the Empire State Building) and uptown (and Central Park).

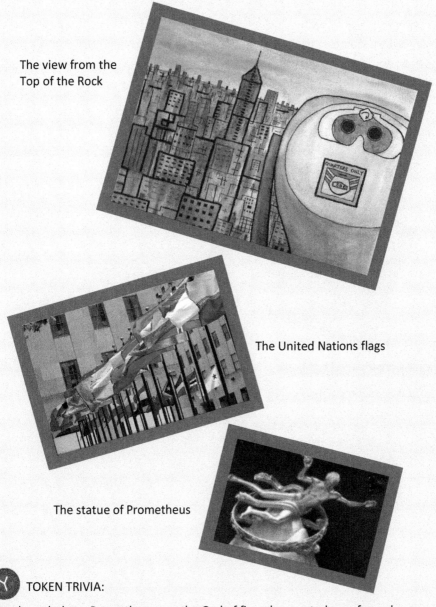

The view from the Top of the Rock

The United Nations flags

The statue of Prometheus

TOKEN TRIVIA:

In Greek mythology, Prometheus was the God of fire who created man from clay.

British Intelligence ran their top-secret operations on the 35th and 36th floors during World War II.

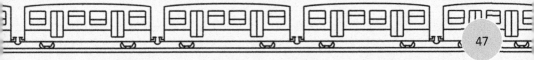

One of New York's most treasured traditions began during the building of Rockefeller Center. In 1931, the construction workers put up a 20-foot Christmas tree on the job site. They decorated it with the few materials they could find—tin cans and chains of scrap paper and cranberries.

The ceremony returned in 1933, this time with an official tree lighting ceremony. Over the years, the decorations have grown to include 30,000 lights and a glistening star on top. Today, the Rockefeller Center Tree Lighting marks the unofficial start of the holiday season.

Every year, Rockefeller Center has a very special job opening.

HELP WANTED

GO FROM FIR TO FABULOUS!

Interested in relocating to NYC?

If you are an evergreen, 75-90 feet tall, this job is for you!

Must be willing to be decorated with over five miles of lights, and wear a star on top 24/7.

Spend the season watching ice skaters at your feet! Get some quality time with Prometheus!

Please note: only trees okay with being turned into mulch come January need apply.

No place means "theater" more than Broadway. It is not just a street in New York: it's the busiest and brightest neighborhood of theaters in the world. In fact, the area got its nickname, "the Great White Way," because of all the dazzle and excitement that makes up the district. In the world of theater, Broadway takes center stage.

Of course, theater as an art had been around for a long time. But in the early 1900s, changes were taking place and New York set the stage for a new type of theater experience. Until then, orchestras played music to entertain the audience during intermission.

A new kind of entertainment, vaudeville, used music *throughout* the performances and audiences loved it. Soon, artists were creating shows that featured new music and catchy tunes. It paved the way for Broadway's greatest production: the musical!

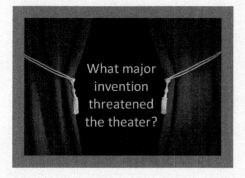

What major invention threatened the theater?

TOKEN TRIVIA:

In the 1800s, stage actors began to become popular for their talent and personalities. One performer who was making a name for himself was John Wilkes Booth. Do you know what made him *really* famous?

The longest running play is *The Phantom of the Opera*, which has had over 900 performances. Over 250 pounds of dry ice are used in each performance. It takes two hours for the actor playing the Phantom to have his makeup applied.

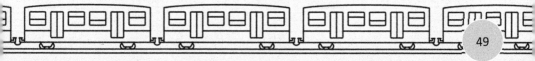

RADIO CITY MUSIC HALL

When Rockefeller designed his office buildings (you remember the name of the place, don't you?), he wanted to include a theater. He believed such a place would bring the best entertainment to the people of New York. That place was to become Radio City Music Hall, the largest indoor theater in the world.

More than 300 million people have visited the theater to enjoy stage and radio shows, concerts, movies, and sporting events.

For over 80 years, the Radio City Christmas Spectacular has been a holiday tradition. The show features the dance company, the Rockettes, who perform many of the same popular acts that were in the show in the 1930s.

The theater itself is renowned for its architecture and stage design.

There are elevators and turntables built into the stage for shows with special effects, and more than 25,000 lights.

A special Wurlitzer organ was built for the theater and has so many pipes it takes up eleven rooms!

You can tour Radio City and see the orchestra pit, the famous Wurlitzer organ (with pipes as high as thirty-two feet), the Rockettes' dressing room, and you can even meet one of the dancers.

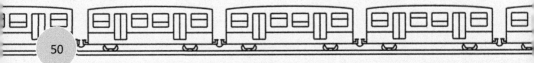

NEW YORK CITY BALLET (NYCB)

The NYCB started over sixty years ago when George Balanchine and Lincoln Kirstein wanted a place for professional dancers to work with promising American students. At the time, there was no such place in the country, especially one that offered the fresh and imaginative style Balanchine and Kirstein imagined.

A performance of George Balanchine's *Symphony in C*

Today, the NYCB has about ninety dancers who perform in the fall, winter, and spring seasons in New York. The school also offers programs for the public, where children can learn about current productions, watch short performances, meet the dancers, and even join them in the studio for warm-up exercises.

A performance of Jerome Robbins' *Glass Pieces*

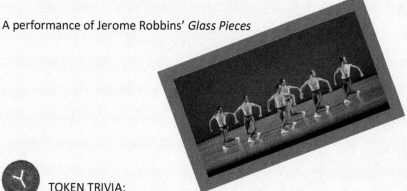

 TOKEN TRIVIA:

One of the most popular performances in the NYCB's repertoire is the annual *Nutcracker*. It has been part of New York's annual holiday traditions since 1954.

The snow that falls in each performance of the *Nutcracker* is actually fifty pounds of confetti.

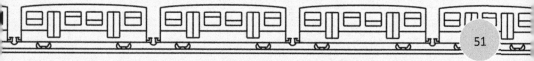

BIG APPLE CIRCUS

Be prepared for an exciting experience when you go to the Big Apple Circus. This is not your average circus show. Yes, you will see jugglers, horses, funny dogs, magicians and contortionists, but they will all perform in ways you have never seen before.

On top of that, the show is performed in one ring. That means everyone watching the show is close to the performers and their stunts. Don't be surprised if one of the clowns tries to eat your popcorn.

Don't try these at home!

The Big Apple Circus began with two jugglers in the 1970s who wanted to try something different. Not only did they want to change the way the public experienced the circus, but they wanted to share the fun with people not at the show. The Big Apple Circus works with schools, under-privileged communities, and children's hospitals to share the magic of the circus.

 TOKEN TRIVIA:

Two performers from the Big Apple Circus are also in the Guinness Book of World Records—at the same time, Pedro Carrillo skipped rope on a high wire 1,323 times while Alesya Gulevich spun 99 hula hoops.

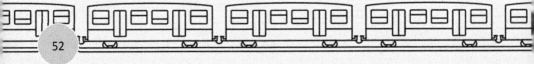

MUSEUM OF THE MOVING IMAGE

The Museum of the Moving Image is not your usual museum. Here, it's all about hands-on playtime, where you can explore old video games systems, learn how to record sound effects and voice-overs, and try your hand at stop- motion animation.

Yoda

Early projectors

ADR (Automated Dialogue Replacement)

Animation station

Displays of licensed merchandise

Arcade games through the years

Central Park is 843 acres (that's the size of 870 football fields!) of open space in the middle of Manhattan. Within the park are museums, lakes, a zoo, and carousel. At the western corner of the park is Strawberry Fields, an area dedicated to the memory of John Lennon.

When the park opened in 1857, it was the first planned city park in the country. For the first time, New Yorkers didn't have to leave the city to enjoy the outdoors.

It wasn't until train service expanded throughout the city that most people could travel so far north and visit the park.

Today, more than 35 million people visit the park each year.

 TOKEN TRIVIA:

For one week in 2001, a two-foot alligator ran loose in the park. It was finally found in Harlem Meer and identified as a caiman. This South American "tourist" was named "Damon the caiman."

More than 5 million pounds of trash is collected in the park every year.

Long ago, it was illegal to sit on the grass in the park.

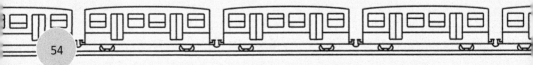

See if you can find these statues in Central Park:

Okay, it's not a needle and it wasn't Cleopatra's, but it's called Cleopatra's Needle anyway. This obelisk is almost 3,500 years old! Obelisks (a word that comes from the Greek *obeliskos* meaning "needle") were built in pairs to honor gods and ward off danger. Egypt sent this one to America in 1877 (the other one is in London).

The statue is covered in hieroglyphics that show the monument had more to do with Egyptian dynasties around 1400 BC (whose rulers wanted their names and achievements carved in stone). Still, it's named for Cleopatra name, probably because the Obelisk of Pharaoh Thutmose III and Ramses II doesn't sound as catchy.

The Balto statue honors the sled dog that prevented the 1925 diphtheria epidemic. The contagious disease was diagnosed in Nome, Alaska, and the city quickly ran out of anti-serum that would prevent its spread. The weather was so bad, there was no way to deliver more medicine.

Balto and the other sled dogs pulled it off though, traveling in a blizzard to deliver the medication. The trip was expected to take thirteen days, but the dogs braved the storm and made it in under six days!

If you know the story of Alice in Wonderland then you'll recognize this statue. On it Alice sits on a mushroom with the White Rabbit, Cheshire Cat, Dormouse, and Mad Hatter.

The opening lines to Carroll's *The Jabberwocky* are engraved at the bottom. "'Twas brillig, and the slithy toves did gyre and gimble in the wabe." Don't worry if you don't understand it; Alice didn't either.

PROSPECT PARK

Prospect Park has seen a lot of change since it was designed in the 1860s. Back then, Brooklyn was a suburb of Manhattan and there was still farmland to be found throughout the area. And before that, the area was the site of a Revolutionary War battle.

Today, Prospect Park sits in the middle of a borough of over 2.5 million people, surrounded by highways, apartment buildings, and row houses.

The 585 acres of Prospect Park feel anything but crowded though. There is a zoo, an ice skating rink, plenty of playgrounds, a carousel, a lake, and gardens to attract all the people who want to enjoy time outdoors.

Also in the park is Lefferts House, where you can see what life was like in the 1700s. The house was destroyed during the Revolutionary War, but was rebuilt by the Lefferts family shortly thereafter.

Lefferts House

Smack in the middle of the West Side (okay, above it) is this elevated park thirty feet above the streets below. You can still see the railroad tracks from a bygone era.

In the 1930s, the city raised the train tracks that ran through the neighborhood. There had been so many accidents between freight trains and the residents that the area earned the nickname "Death Avenue."

The old train tracks

By the 1980s, trains stopped running on these lines, and the area fell into disrepair. Not long after, there were plans calling for its demolition. The community worked together to turn it into a park. The result of their creativity and dedication is a High Line: a mile-long terrace of gardens and paths, deliciously connected to the Chelsea Market. There is no better place to grab lunch on a nice day.

PARKS WHERE YOU CAN FIND A CAROUSEL:

- Central Park's Friedsam Memorial Carousel
- Bryant Park's Le Carrousel
- Riverbank State Park Carousel
- The Carousel at Pier 62
- SeaGlass Carousel at Battery Park
- Prospect Park

PARKS WHERE YOU CAN ICE SKATE:

- Bank of America Winter Village at Bryant Park
- Trump Lasker Rink and Wollman Rink in Central Park
- Brookfield Place Winter Garden
- Rockefeller Center Rink
- Sky Rink at Chelsea Piers
- Riverbank State Park

There are few walks in New York as beautiful as the one across the Brooklyn Bridge. This suspension bridge over the East River connects Manhattan to Brooklyn.

When the bridge first opened in 1883, the two locales were still separate cities, and it was the first steel-wire suspension bridge in the world. The bridge's towers were the tallest in America and its 1,595-foot span was the longest.

The engineer, Washington Roebling, knew he had a hard job ahead of him when he started construction. (His late father had designed it. Talk about pressure!).

Roebling decided to use steel and add trusses beneath the span. His ideas gave extra support to the structure, so that it could withstand strong winds and added weight on the roadway.

The trusses under the bridge

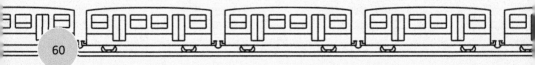

Building a bridge is be a dangerous job. Sadly, one risk went unnoticed until it started affecting many workers, even Roebling himself.

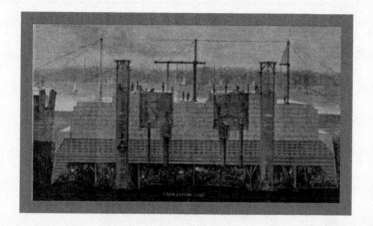

To build the foundation for the bridge, workers had to work in the river. They worked underwater in caissons as they dug their way into the bedrock. Even though the caissons were filled with compressed air, the danger came when it was time for the men to return to the surface.

Leaving the caisson too quickly caused gas bubbles to build up in a worker's body. The result was an awful condition called "caisson disease," or "the bends." Workers with the bends suffered blindness, paralysis, horrible joint pain, breathing difficulty, and even death.

Once the cause was discovered, it was easy to control. Workers had to rise slowly to give their bodies time to adjust to the change in pressure.

 TOKEN TRIVIA:

When the bridge first opened, the toll was one penny. Today, it's free!

In 1901, a man named William McCloundy was sent to prison for selling the Brooklyn Bridge to a tourist!

Even today, peregrine falcons nest on top of the bridge.

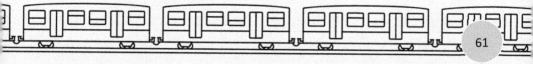

The *Intrepid* is a decommissioned aircraft carrier from World War II that is now a sea-air-space museum.

The *Intrepid* has been one busy ship. She fought in so many battles in World War Two, she earned the nickname "the Fighting 1." Years later, the ship served in the Vietnam War and then worked as a submarine surveillance vessel. In later years, the ship even recovered space capsules after two NASA missions.

At the Space Shuttle Pavilion, you can see the *Enterprise.* It's hard to believe that it was delivered to New York <u>on top</u> of a 747!

You can examine a Concorde SST (which flew from New York to Europe in under three hours!) and a Lockheed Blackbird (the world's fastest plane). Then climb into the *USS Growler* and feel what life was like on a submarine (clue: it wasn't the most spacious of quarters).

 TOKEN TRIVIA:

In 2006, the *Intrepid* needed to be moved for repairs and restoration. The Coast Guard wasn't able to move her for three weeks. There was so much mud and silt around her that she was stuck and needed to be dug out!

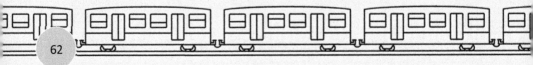

STATEN ISLAND FERRY

The Staten Island Ferry takes people between Staten Island and Manhattan, and has been doing it 24 hours a day, 365 days a year for over 100 years.

The half-hour trip between Whitehall Terminal in Manhattan and St. George Terminal on Staten Island offers some of the best views of NYC, including those of Ellis Island, the Statue of Liberty, and the Brooklyn Bridge. It's a crowded ride during rush hour, so if you want a seat make sure to go during a quieter time.

 TOKEN TRIVIA:

The ferry is actually a fleet of eight ferries.

When the ferry first opened in 1817, it cost 25 cents to ride. In 1897, it was lowered to 5 cents. Today, it's free!

The ferries are a deep orange color to be easy to spot in bad weather.

At one time, some of the ferries were used as prisons.

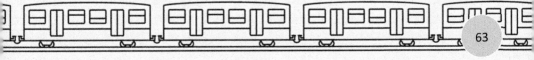

Having over 600 species of animals roaming, swimming, and stirring over 250 acres makes the Bronx Zoo the largest in the world. Here, you can discover what kind of cockroach makes a good pet, and then stop by the gorilla quarters and look for the silverback. Be sure to make time to watch how tiger cubs play with their siblings—it might remind you of your own house.

Since the zoo opened in 1899, its ambition has always been to "save wildlife" and educate the public about the animal world. It was one of the first zoos that believed animals would rather spend their time roaming, playing, and exploring than sitting in a cage. You'll see this in the Congo Gorilla Forest, Tiger Mountain, Madagascar!, the African Plains, and Wild Asia. Some exhibits are so natural that predators and prey have been placed together (but just to make sure life for the animals doesn't get too wild, the exhibits have moats).

The zoo has always been wild about animals. In the early 1900s, it took in American bison, an animal that was close to becoming extinct. After helping get government protection for the bison, the zoo spent years growing the herd. The zoo was so successful that it was able to return hundreds of bison to their natural (now protected) habitat throughout the Western US—a number today that reaches over 20,000!

THE BRONX ZOO

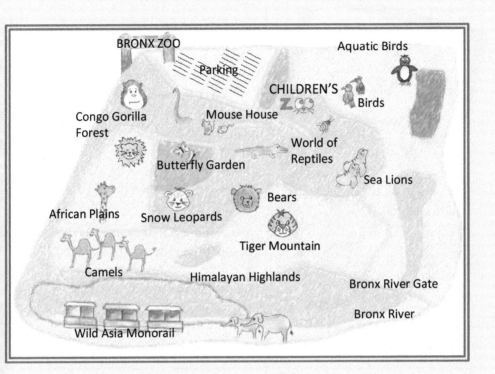

BRONX ZOO

Parking

Aquatic Birds

CHILDREN'S ZOO

Birds

Congo Gorilla Forest

Mouse House

World of Reptiles

Butterfly Garden

Sea Lions

African Plains

Snow Leopards

Bears

Tiger Mountain

Camels

Himalayan Highlands

Bronx River Gate

Bronx River

Wild Asia Monorail

Do you know:

With all the animals roaming around, what famous resident isn't able to move?

Which animal was rescued from a landslide and brought to the zoo to live?

Are gorillas herbivores, carnivores, or omnivores? And what do those terms mean anyway?

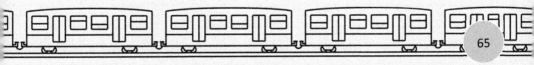

Back in the 1850s, when a local man gave a bear cub to a park employee, there was not even any talk of having a park zoo. But as more people began donating animals, a zoo started to take shape (if for no other reason than to have a place to keep all the animals). Can you guess the strangest donation? A "tiglon" came to the park in the 1930s. It was a cross between an African lion and a Siberian tiger.

Now, the Central Park Zoo has grown to 6.5 acres with habitats and animals from tropical rainforests, the polar region, and temperate climates.

While a lot of the zoo has been remodeled (like the Tisch Children's Zoo), there are still some popular remnants from past years. The sea lion pool remains at the center of the zoo, where it's been since the 1930s. Whether you visit during their meal times or not, the sea lions always enjoy showing off for visitors.

Just outside the zoo is the much-loved George Delacorte Musical Clock. It plays music on the hour and half-hour, with a band of animal sculptures playing along with their instruments. If you go during the holidays, you'll be able to hear their seasonal melodies.

NEW YORK PUBLIC LIBRARY

The city's most famous lions sit at the entrance to the Public Library on Fifth Avenue.

Patience sits on the south side.

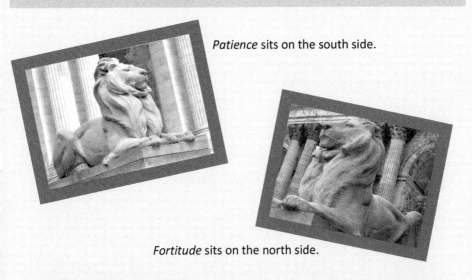

Fortitude sits on the north side.

Yep, it's the real deal. Winnie the Pooh, after many much-loved years with his owner, Christopher Robin Milne, now lives at the New York Public Library. You can visit the bear and his friends, Eeyore, Piglet, Tigger, and Kanga, at the Stephen A. Schwarzman Building.

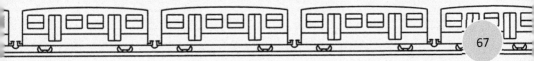

New Yorkers love their sports. The city has two major baseball teams, two football teams, three basketball teams, and an ice hockey team (with another on the way). New York also has a soccer team, the New York Red Bulls, and plays host to the tennis US Open and the NYC Marathon.

While all the teams have loyal fans, it's baseball that seems to stir up the excitement year after year. With teams like the Yankees and the Mets, it's no wonder New Yorkers look forward to opening day each spring.

Back in 1903, the Highlanders were the baseball team in New York. They changed their name to the Yankees in 1913 and went on to be called "baseball's greatest team" and win twenty-seven World Series!

Some of the best players in history have played for the Yankees: Babe Ruth, Lou Gehrig, Joe DiMaggio, Mickey Mantle, Roger Maris, Reggie Jackson, Don Mattingly, Thurman Munson, Roger Clemens, and Jason Giambi.

New York welcomed the Mets to the city in 1962.

Over the years, the team has had some great players, including Willie Mays, Tom Seaver, and Darryl Strawberry.

The Mets have won two world championships. The city was even more consumed by baseball in 2000, when the Mets faced the Yankees in the World Series (the Yankees won 4-1).

There is a never-ending rivalry between New York and Boston sports teams. In baseball, it's the Yankees and the Red Sox who have been battling it out for over a hundred years. In basketball, the battle is between the NY Knicks and the Boston Celtics, and it has been going on for over sixty years. The rivalry has taken them to fourteen playoffs.

The Knicks have shown their strength in the league, not only by winning the NBA championships but by making it to the postseason forty-two times!

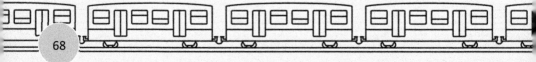

The Giants football team might have their stadium in New Jersey, but they are still the team of New York. They are one of the oldest teams in the NFL, having been around since 1925. Over the years, they have won four Super Bowl titles (and eight wins if you count the years before the playoffs began in 1970).

Being that high up in the rankings makes them a serious opponent and, while a lot of discussion goes into which rivalries matter, most people would agree that the Giants and the Philadelphia Eagles have one of the fiercest—and the longest running. The teams started battling it out in 1933 and haven't let up since.

People like to talk about the Giants-Jets intra-city matchup as one that's very intense. While there is some competition, it's hard to take it too seriously when you share the same stadium and play in different conferences. While the two teams might meet each other once in a while throughout the season, most of their contact comes in pre-season games.

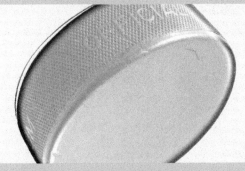

Watch the New York Rangers once and you'll be hooked! They have won the Stanley Cup four times (in fact, they were the first American team in the NHL to do so), and that number might change very soon. They went through some long-term dry spells and setbacks but that all seems to be a thing of the past. It looks like they are ready to power forward.

How well do you know your NY teams? See if you know which of these is true or false.

1. The real name of the city's basketball team is the New York City Knickers.

2. The Knicks are one of only two teams still playing in their original cities.

3. The first game played in Yankee Stadium was against the Boston Red Sox in 1923.

4. The Yankees have had the following players in their famous history: Babe Ruth, Lou Gehrig, Joe DiMaggio, Mickey Mantle, Reggie Jackson, Tom Seaver, and Darryl Strawberry.

5. Madison Square Garden is built over Grand Central Terminal.

6. Citi Field is the home of the NY Mets. The old stadium was called Shea Stadium.

7. Both football teams, the Jets and the Giants, play their home games in stadiums across the street from one another.

8. The Rangers were originally supposed to be called the Giants.

9. The Mets took their team colors, blue and orange, in honor of two other teams.

10. Before the Giants football team got their own stadium, they played their home games at Yankee Stadium.

11. Green and white are the colors the Jets wear now, but the team colors were once blue and gold.

12. The Rangers brought the sport of ice hockey to NYC.

 TOKEN TRIVIA:

The Knicks and the Rangers play at Madison Square Garden, which isn't actually a square or a garden. It's a circular arena in midtown that hosts a lot of sporting events.

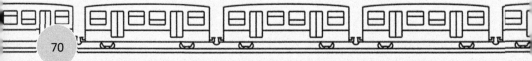

'TIS THE SEASON

These special events only happen once a year. Be sure to see them if you get a chance.

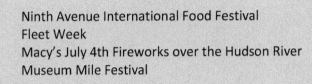

Ninth Avenue International Food Festival
Fleet Week
Macy's July 4th Fireworks over the Hudson River
Museum Mile Festival

San Gennaro Feast in Little Italy
Columbus Day Parade

Macy's Thanksgiving Day Parade
Rockefeller Center Tree Lighting
Lunar New Year Parade in Chinatown
St. Patrick's Day Parade

Easter Parade on Fifth Avenue
Opening Day for the start of the Baseball Season
Ninth Avenue Food Festival

WHERE IN NEW YORK WOULD YOU FIND THESE?

After your visit, see if you can match these!

 A.

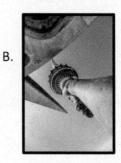 B.

 C.

 D.

 E.

 F.

 G.

 H.

1. Intrepid Museum

2. Bronx Zoo

3. Central Park

4. Statue of Liberty

5. Public Library

6. Subway

7. Rockefeller Center

8. Federal Reserve

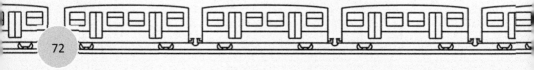

P. 7 - The Macy's Thanksgiving Day Parade uses several hundreds of thousands cubic feet of helium for its balloons

P. 13 - The Empire State Building

P. 15 - A terminal is where trains begin and end their routes. A station is where trains stop along their routes to allow passengers and good on and off.

P. 18 - Thirty

P. 20 - Since 1774, our country has had nine capitals: Philadelphia; Baltimore, MD; Lancaster, PA; York, PA; Princeton, NJ; Annapolis, MD; Trenton, NJ; New York City; and, finally, Washington, DC.

P. 36 - 1) C, 2) D, 3) F, 4) A, 5) G, 6) B, 7) E

P. 37 - It hung upside down for 47 days until someone noticed the mistake.

P. 39 - His name was Alexander Eiffel and he designed the Eiffel Tower

P. 40 - King Kong

P. 49 - John Wilkes Booth killed President Abraham Lincoln in 1865—while Lincoln was at the theater watching a show! With the advent of sound in motion pictures, people started going to movies more often than the theater.

P. 65 - The Rocking Stone, a thirty-ton pink granite relic from the Ice Age. Leo, a snow leopard from Pakistan. Herbivores, meaning they eat plants. Carnivores eat meat and omnivores aren't picky: they eat everything and anything.

P. 70 - 1) False. It's the Knickerbockers. 2) True. The other team is the Boston Celtics. 3) True. Babe Ruth hit three home runs and the Yankees won. 4) False. Seaver and Strawberry played for the Mets. 5) False. It stands over Penn Station. 6) True. 7) False. They both play in Giants Stadium, recently renamed MetLife Stadium. 8) True. 9) True. The Mets replaced the two local National League teams, the Brooklyn Dodgers (the blue) and the New York Giants (the orange). 10) True. 11) True. 12) False. Before the Rangers, NYC had another team, the New York Americans. They played from 1925-1942.

P. 72 - 1) F, 2) D, 3) A, 4) B, 5) G, 6) H, 7) E, 8) C

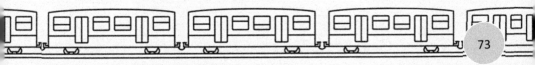

GLOSSARY

Caisson— French for "big box." These were watertight, wooden chambers used by construction workers underwater

Chutzpah— Yiddish slang for determination and courage

Currency— Money used in a particular country

Decommissioned— No longer in service

Dirigible— A lightweight aircraft that is guided by a propeller (like a blimp)

Hieroglyphics— Ancient writing using pictures instead of words

Immigrant— A person who moves to a new country to live

Knish— A dumpling made of dough and filled with ingredients such as ground beef or mashed potatoes

lightning rod— A pole on top of a building that prevents lightning from hitting the building by carrying the electrical charge to the ground

Meteorite— Rock, or a similar object, that falls from space to earth

Obelisk— A stone monument with a pyramid shape on the top

Onassis— Jacqueline Kennedy. The wife of President John F. Kennedy

Parapet— a low wall that surrounds an elevated structure such as a roof

Quarantine— To separate an ill person until they recover so that they don't pass their illness on to others

Steerage— People who had the cheapest tickets for their passage. They had to stay on the lowest decks of the ship

Tenement— A house or building where several families live. Tenement buildings were very often crowded and run down

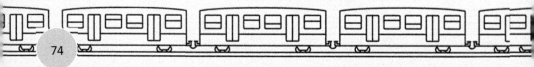

LOCATION, LOCATION, LOCATION

American Museum of Natural History - 79th Street and Central Park West - www.amnh.org

Big Apple Circus - www.bigapplecircus.org

Bronx Zoo - www.bronxzoo.com

Central Park - 59th to 110th Street between Fifth Avenue and Central Park West - www.centralparknyc.org

Central Park Zoo - 64th Street and Fifth Avenue - www.centralparkzoo.com

Chrysler Building - 405 Lexington Avenue

Ellis Island - www.nps.gov

Empire State Building - 350 Fifth Avenue - www.esbnyc.com

FAO Schwarz - Fifth Avenue at 58th Street

Flatiron Building - 175 Fifth Avenue

Grand Central Terminal - 89 East 42nd Street

Highline Park - Gansevoort Street to 34th Street between 10th and 12th Avenues- www.thehighline.org

Intrepid - Pier 86 at 12th Avenue and 46th Street - www.intrepidmuseum.org

Merchant's House - 29 East 4th Street - www.merchantshouse.org

Metropolitan Museum of Art - 1000 Fifth Avenue - www.metmuseum.org

Museum of Modern Art - 11 West 53rd Street - www.moma.org

Museum of the Moving Image - 36-01 35th Avenue, Queens - www.movingimage.us/

New York City Ballet - www.nycballet.com

New York Public Library - 455 Fifth Avenue - www.nypl.org

One World Trade Center - www.onewtc.com

Prospect Park - www.prospectpark.org

Radio City Music Hall - 1260 6th Avenue - www.radiocity.com

Rockefeller Center - Fifth Avenue between 47th and 50th Streets - www.rockefellercenter.com

Staten Island Ferry - www.siferry.com

Statue of Liberty - www.nps.gov

Tenement Museum - 97 Orchard Street - www.tenement.org

Times Square - www.timessquarenyc.org

Trinity Church - 75 Broadway - www.trinitywallstreet.org

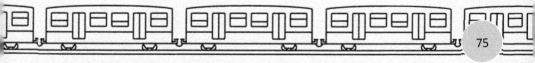

I'LL BE READING YOU

If you want to read more about New York City, try some of these books:

A Cricket in Times Square by George Selden
Eloise by Kay Thompson
From the Mixed-Up Files of Mrs. Basil E. Frankweiler by E.L. Konigsburg
In the Night Kitchen by Maurice Sendak
Stuart Little by E.B. White
The Curious Garden by Peter Brown
The Snowy Day by Ezra Jack Keats

Books of Wonder is a world of books just for kids.

Photo Credits

The author wishes to thank the following people, institutions, and organizations for providing artwork and images for this book.

American Museum of Natural History - 30; 32; 33 (all D. Finnin). **Big Apple Circus** -52 (all Bertrand Guay) **Books of Wonder** - 76. **Creative Commons** - 33. **Intrepid Sea, Air & Space Museum** - 62. **Library of Congress Prints and Photographs Division** - 10b; 13b (Carol D. Highsmith Archive Collection); 14; 18 (b,Highsmith Collection); 19t; 20t; 26r; 27r; 28tl; 36 (Highsmith Collection); 38r; 41l (Highsmith Collection); 50 (Highsmith Collection); 61. **Merchant's House Museum** - 25. **Metropolitan Museum of Art, New York** - 34; 35. **Mumford, Kelly** - inside cover; 6c; 47t; 60t; 63t. **Museum of Modern Art** - 2013 Artists Rights Society (ARS); New York/Pro Litteris, Zurich. **Museum of the Moving Image** - Brian Palmer 53 (tl); Peter Aaron/Esto (cl, tr, bl); Stefan Hagen (cr, br). **NASA** - 30b. **National Park Service** - 22 (all); 23 (all photos). **New York City Ballet** - 51 (Paul Kolnik). **New York Public Library** - 15b; 19b; 20b; 28bl; 42r. **istock** - 6 (all photos); 8; 10t; 11; 12; 13t; 15t; 16b; 17; 23r; 26l; 27l; 28r; 29; 31l; 38l; 39; 41r; 44; 45; 46; 47c; 48r, tl; 49; 54l, r; 55t, b; 56; 58l; 59; 60b; 63b; 64b; 66t,c; 68, 69; 72; 73; subway token image; back cover. **Prospect Park Alliance** - 57. **Publicdomainpictures.net** - 33. **Roche** - 26; 47; 48; 58; 62; 66; 67; 71. **Skyscraper Museum** - 42; 43. **Tenement Museum** - 24. **Wikimedia Commons** - 31 (Renzokuken, LH; Torres Jr., Daniel); 55 (Uris); 71 (Young, R). **Wildlife Conservation Society** - 64 (Julie Larsen Maher). And **Dominic Flask** for his graphic designs used throughout the book

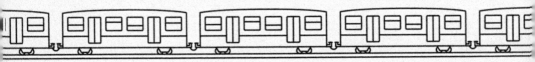

CPSIA information can be obtained
at www.ICGtesting.com
Printed in the USA
LVOW05s1619230616

493836LV00047B/261/P